CAMBRIDGE LIBRARY COLLECTION

Books of enduring scholarly value

History

The books reissued in this series include accounts of historical events and movements by eye-witnesses and contemporaries, as well as landmark studies that assembled significant source materials or developed new historiographical methods. The series includes work in social, political and military history on a wide range of periods and regions, giving modern scholars ready access to influential publications of the past.

Observations on the Reflections of Edmund Burke on the Revolution in France

Catharine Macaulay (1731–91) is considered to have been the first female historian. Her eight-volume *History of England* (1763–83) and her radical views brought her considerable fame in eighteenth-century England. She was a political activist in favour of parliamentary reform, and wrote several political pamphlets on the subject. She also wrote the feminist work *Letters on Education* (1790), which argues for the equal education of men and women and is thought to have been influential upon Mary Wollstonecraft. Macaulay supported both the American Revolution and the French Revolution and saw them as moves towards equality and liberty. This political pamphlet, first published in 1790, was written in support of the French Revolution and against Burke's *Reflections on the Revolution in France*. It is a passionate polemic that challenges Burke's interpretation of British history. It remains an important work in the history of political philosophy.

T0364270

Cambridge University Press has long been a pioneer in the reissuing of out-of-print titles from its own backlist, producing digital reprints of books that are still sought after by scholars and students but could not be reprinted economically using traditional technology. The Cambridge Library Collection extends this activity to a wider range of books which are still of importance to researchers and professionals, either for the source material they contain, or as landmarks in the history of their academic discipline.

Drawing from the world-renowned collections in the Cambridge University Library and other partner libraries, and guided by the advice of experts in each subject area, Cambridge University Press is using state-of-the-art scanning machines in its own Printing House to capture the content of each book selected for inclusion. The files are processed to give a consistently clear, crisp image, and the books finished to the high quality standard for which the Press is recognised around the world. The latest print-on-demand technology ensures that the books will remain available indefinitely, and that orders for single or multiple copies can quickly be supplied.

The Cambridge Library Collection brings back to life books of enduring scholarly value (including out-of-copyright works originally issued by other publishers) across a wide range of disciplines in the humanities and social sciences and in science and technology.

Observations on the Reflections of Edmund Burke on the Revolution in France

CATHARINE MACAULAY

CAMBRIDGE UNIVERSITY PRESS

Cambridge, New York, Melbourne, Madrid, Cape Town,
Singapore, São Paolo, Delhi, Mexico City

Published in the United States of America by Cambridge University Press, New York

www.cambridge.org
Information on this title: www.cambridge.org/9781108045407

© in this compilation Cambridge University Press 2012

This edition first published 1790
This digitally printed version 2012

ISBN 978-1-108-04540-7 Paperback

OBSERVATIONS

ON THE

REFLECTIONS

OF THE

Right Hon. EDMUND BURKE,

ON THE

REVOLUTION in FRANCE,

IN A LETTER TO THE

Right Hon. the EARL of STANHOPE.

———————

LONDON:

PRINTED FOR C. DILLY, IN THE POULTRY.

M,DCC,XC.

OBSERVATIONS, &c.

My Lord,

YOUR lordſhip's character as a patriot, a philoſopher, and the firm friend of the general rights of man, encourages me to pre-ſent to you the following Obſervations on Mr. Burke's famous Reflections on the Revolution in France. They claim no popular attention for the ornaments of ſtile in which they are delivered; they can attract no admiration from the faſcinating charms of eloquence; they are directed, not to *captivate*, but to *con-vince*; and it is on the preſumption that your lordſhip attends more to the *ſubſtance* and *end* of literary compoſitions, than to the *art* of their arrangement, which induces me to flatter myſelf with your approbation.

B   It

It is not furprizing that an event, the moft
important to the deareft interefts of mankind,
the moft *fingular* in its nature, and the moft
aftonifhing in its means, fhould not only have
attracted the curiofity of all civilized nations,
but that it fhould have engaged the paffions
of all *reflecting* men.

Two parties are already formed in this
country, who behold the French Revolution
with a very oppofite temper: to the one, it
infpires the fentiments of *exultation* and *rapture;* and to the other, *indignation* and *fcorn*.
I fhall not take upon me to confider what are
the *fecret* paffions which have given birth to
thefe laft fentiments; and fhall content myfelf
with obferving, that Mr. Burke has undertaken to be the oracle of this laft party. The
abilities of this gentleman have been fully acknowledged by the impatience with which
the public have waited for his obfervations;
and when we confider that he has been in a
manner educated in the great fchool of Parliament, that he has affifted in the public
councils of the Englifh nation for the greater
part of his life, we muft fuppofe him fully
competent to the tafk he has undertaken, of
cenfuring

cenfuring the politics of our neighbour kingdom, and entering into an exact definition
of thofe native rights which equally attach
themfelves to every defcription of men.

Is there a rational obfervation, or argument, in moral exiftence, which this gentleman (fo highly favoured by nature and circumftances for political debate) could poffibly
have paffed over, on a fubject in which he
appears fo greatly interefted, and of which he
has taken a full leifure to confider. When
we find him then *obliged* to fubftitute a *warm*
and *paffionate declamation* to a *cool inveftiga-
tion*, and to addrefs the *paffions* inftead of
the *reafon* of mankind, we fhall be induced
to give a fuller credit to our judgment and
our feelings, in the view we have taken of
this interefting object, and the pleafure it has
given us.

Mr. Burke fets out with throwing a *great
deal* of contemptuous cenfure on two club focieties in London, for a very harmlefs exertion of natural and conftitutional liberty.
They certainly had a right to compliment the
French National Affembly on a matter of do-
meftic government, and to exprefs an *appro-*

bation

bation of their conduct, with a freedom equal to that which Mr. Burke has taken in his letter to exprefs his *abhorrence.*

The National Affembly of France have taken no fuch *fupercilious ftate* upon them, as would render fuch a communication of fentiment ridiculous or prefumptuous. As the patrons of *equal liberty,* they have not difdained the addreffes of the *meaneft* individual : confequently the Revolution Society then might rationally expect that their addrefs would have met with a civil reception, though not clothed with the " dignity of the whole reprefentative majefty of the whole Englifh nation."

But Mr. Burke thinks that thefe gentlemen have fo ftrong a predilection in favour of the democratic arrangements which have taken place in France, that they have been induced to wifh, if not to indulge an hope, that fome very important reformations may in the procefs of time alfo take place in this country ; and thefe harmlefs operations of the mind in a *few obfcure* individuals (for fuch are the members defcribed who compofe the offending clubs) have produced in Mr. Burke apprehenfions

prehenfions no ways confiftent with the *high* opinion he has formed of the Englifh conftitution, or of the *ftrong* attachment which he fuppofes all that is *great* and *good* in the nation have to it.

Dr. Price, whofe animated love for mankind and the fpread of general happinefs moved to exprefs the effufion of his patriotic fentiment, in a fermon preached the 4th of Nov. 1789, at the diffenting meeting-houfe in the Old Jewry, is cenfured by Mr. Burke in *fevere*, and even *acrimonious terms.* Among other parts of the very offenfive matter with which he charges this fermon, the having afferted that the *King of Great Britain owes his right to the Crown by the choice of the people*, is particularly felected, as worthy an hiftorical and argumentative confutation.

The liberty that was taken in the year 1688, by a convention of Lords and Commons, to depofe king James the reigning fovereign from the throne, and to veft the fovereignty of the realm in his daughter Mary, and her hufband the prince of Orange ; and afterwards by the legiflature, to pafs an act to fettle the fucceffion in queen

Anne

Anne and her iffue, and in default of thefe, in the heirs of king William's body, and in default of thefe, in the houfe of Hanover, (the Proteftant defcendants of the houfe of Stuart in the female line;) and this to the prejudice not only of king James, but of his fon, who had been acknowledged as the lawful heir of his throne; and alfo to the prejudice of the houfe of Savoy, who by lineal defcent were the next in regular fucceffion; are indeed facts, which *might warrant a plain thinking man* in the opinion, that the prefent reigning family owe their fucceffion to the choice or affent of the people. But, in Mr. Burke's opinion, thefe facts are of no weight, " becaufe the whole family of the Stuarts were not entirely left out of the fucceffion, and a native of England advanced to the throne; and becaufe it was declared in the act of fucceffion, that the Proteftant line drawn from James the firft, was abfolutely neceffary for the fecurity of the realm."

That thofe individuals of the family of the Stuarts, who had never committed any offence againft the peace of the country, and whofe mode of faith was not injurious to its welfare,

welfare, fhould not be fet afide in favour of an abfolute ftranger to the blood, was certainly a *juft meafure*; and it was certainly *wife* to leave as *few* competitors to the crown as poffible, whether on grounds founded in juftice, or in mere plaufibility. But there was a reafon ftill more forcible for the conduct of the two Houfes of Convention, and afterwards for the Parliament in their conftitutional capacity; and the reafon is this, that *without the prince of Orange, and the affiftance of his Dutch army, there could have been no Revolution.* For the Englifh nation at large was fo little convinced of the *fevere and grave neceffity* which Mr. Burke talks of, that the people of themfelves would never have been roufed to have depofed king James; and they regarded all his innovations with fuch a *conftitutional phlegm*, that had this unfortunate monarch poffeffed the qualities of *firmnefs, perfeverance*, or *patience*, he muft either have been killed by the dark means of *affaffination*, or he would have *continued on the throne.*

That the friends of the Revolution knew they could not do without the affiftance of

3   king

king William, is plain, by their laying afide
the intention of vefting Mary *fingly* with the
fovereignty, on his declaring that if this
event took place, he would return to Hol-
land, and leave them to themfelves.

However ftrongly the warm friends of
freedom might wifh that this abftract right
of the people, of chufing their own magif-
trates, and depofing them for ill conduct,
had been laid open to the public by a formal
declaration of fuch a right in the acts of fucceffion, this certainly was not a period of
time for carrying thefe wifhes into execution.
The whole body of the people had fwallowed
deeply of the *poifon* of church policy; *paffive
obedience*, by their means, had fo entirely fup-
planted the *abftract notion* of the *rights of men*,
which prevailed in the oppofition to Charles
the firft; and fo defirous were the triumphant
party to prevent the revival of fuch a principle, by which their interefts had been affected,
that they took care to confound the *only juft
authority* they had for their conduct, in as
great *a mift of words and terms as poffible.*
Befides, would William, who was the foul of
the whole proceeding, have given way to a

claim,

claim, by which, in the plaineſt terms, he was bound to his good behaviour?

Mr. Hume juſtly ſuppoſes, that if the revolution had happened one hundred years after it did, it would have been *materially different* in all its circumſtances. Inſtead of thinking with Mr. Burke, that ſuch a plain declaration of the rights of men would have tended to diſturb the quiet of the nation, I firmly believe that it would have had a contrary effect; for, in this caſe, thoſe endleſs diſputes between the *Nonjurors*, *Tories*, and *Whigs*, would ſoon have had an end. For, the queſtion not being involved in that *obſcurity*, *contradiction*, and *abſurdity*, in which it was enveloped by the revolutioniſts, *truth* and *reaſon* would have reſumed their ſway; *party jargon* would have been exploded; the people would have given a chearful obedience to the new government; and that dreadful *neceſſity* by which Sir Robert Walpole excuſed the introducing a ſettled *ſyſtem of corruption* into the adminiſtration, would never have exiſted.

When the ſucceſſion to a crown in one family, or even the poſſeſſion of private property, owes its origin to the people, moſt undoubtedly the authority from whence it's

derived,

derived, attaches itself to the gift as equally in every individual of the family through the whole line of fucceffion, as in the firft poffef-for. And I can hardly believe, that there was *one* enlightened member who compofed part of that legiflative body who fettled the fuc-ceffion to the throne, could poffibly think that body poffeffed of fuch a plenitude of power, as fhould give them a right, not only to *fet afide* the regulations of their anceftors, but to *bind their pofterity*, to all fucceeding generations, in the permanent chains of an unalterable law. Should we once admit of *a power fo incompatible with the conditions of humanity*, and only referved for the dictates of *divine wifdom*, we have not, in thefe en-lightened days, improved on the politics of the fanatic atheift Hobbes : *For he fuppofes an original right in the people to chufe their gover-nors;* but, in exerting this right, the citizen and his pofterity for ever lofe their native privileges, and become bound through the whole feries of generations to the fervice of a mafter's will.

We will now take into confideration the na-ture and tendency of the two different compli-ments which have been paid by Dr. Price and

Mr.

Mr. Burke to his Majesty and his succeſſors. Dr. Price, I think, puts their right to government on the *moſt dignified*, and perhaps, in the event of things, on the *moſt permanent* footing. But Mr. Burke would have done well to conſider, whether ſuch a compliment as he is willing to pay to royalty is at all *proper*, either for the ſubject to make, or the King to receive. To a weak prince, it would be apt to cancel in his mind *all the obligations* which he owes to the people, and, by flattering him in a *vain* conceit of a mere perſonal right, tempt him to break thoſe ſacred ties which ought to *bind* and *direct* his government. I am apt to believe, that almoſt *all the vices* of royal adminiſtration have principally been occaſioned by a *ſlaviſh adulation* in the language of their ſubjects; and, to the *ſhame of the Engliſh people* it muſt be ſpoken, that none of the enſlaved nations in the world addreſs the throne in a more *fulſome* and *hyperbolical* ſtile of ſubmiſſive flattery.

To a *wiſe* and a *good* prince, compliments of the ſame complexion, made and recommended by Mr. Burke, would be *offenſive*. He would conſider it as taking away the *nobleſt* and *ſafeſt title* by which he poſſeſſes his

power;

power: he would confider it as acknowledg-
ing a kind of *latent* right in other families;
and the liberality of his fentiment would in-
cline him to triumph in the opinion, that he
was *called* to government, and *continued* in
it, by the *choice* and *confidence* of a free
nation.

Mr. Burke feems to adopt *prejudice*, *opinion*,
and the powers of the *imagination*, as the *fafeft*
grounds on which *wife* and *good* ftatefmen can
eftablifh or continue the happinefs of focieties.
Thefe have always been imputed by philofo-
phers (a tribe of men whom indeed Mr. Burke
affects much to defpife) as caufes which have
produced all that is *vicious* and *foolifh* in
man, and confequently have been the fruit-
ful fource of human *mifery*.

Mr. Burke has certainly a *fine* imagination;
but I would not advife either *him*, or any of
his admirers, to give *too much* way to fuch di-
rection; for if from the virtue of our nature
it does not lead us into *crimes*, it always in-
volves us in *error*.

The being put into a fituation clearly to
underftand and to obey the *principles of truth*,
appears to be the bafis of our happinefs in this,

and

and our perfection in another world; and the *more* truth is followed and purfued in this dark vale of human ignorance and mifery, the *more* we fhall *encreafe* our mundane felicity, and *fecure* the bleffings of a future exiftence. *Every opinion* which deviates from *truth*, muft ever be a *treacherous* guide; and the more it deviates from it, it becomes the *more dangerous*.

Though a falfe opinion of the rights and powers of citizens may *enflave* the ductile mind into a ftate of paffive obedience, and thus fecure the peace of government; yet in the fame degree does it inflate the *pride* and *arrogance* of princes, until all confiderations of *rectitude* give way to *will*, the barriers of perfonal fecurity are flung down, and thence arifes that *tremendous neceffity* which muft be followed by a ftate of *violence* and *anarchy*, which Mr. Burke fo *juftly* dreads. That this is the cafe, the experience of all focieties of men who acknowledge a *power* in their princes *paramount* to all refiftance, fully evinces. Thefe focieties are obliged often to have recourfe to violence and maffacre; not indeed to eftablifh any popular rights, but

in

in the way of force, to wreck their vengeance on their tyrants.

As to the right of *cashiering* or *depofing* monarchs for mifgovernment, I cannot poffibly agree with Mr. Burke, that in England it only exifted in that Convention of the two Houfes in 1688, which exercifed this power over King James and his legal fucceffors. But I am clearly of opinion, that it is a right that ought *never* to be exercifed by a people who are fatisfied with their form of government, and have fpirit enough to correct its abufes ; and fo far from *condemning* the French nation for not depofing or executing their king, even though the *ftrongeft prefump-tions* of the *moft atrocious guilt* fhould have appeared againft him, I think, had they elected any other perfon to that high office, they would have thrown difficulties in the way of their liberty, inftead of improving it. But it is the *wifdom*, and not the *folly* of the National Affembly, which gives *offence* to their *enemies ;* and *forces even Mr. Burke* to contradict, in this inftance, the rule which he has laid down, " That monarchs fhould not be depofed for mifconduct, but only when

I   its

its criminality is of a kind to render their government totally incompatible with the safety of the people."

But before we leave the subject of Dr. Price's patriotic effusions, we must take notice of a very heavy charge laid against him by Mr. Burke—no less than that of *prophaning* the beautiful and prophetic ejaculation, commonly called, *Nunc dimittis*! made on the first proclamation of our Saviour in the Temple, and applying it, " *with an inhuman and unnatural rapture, to the most horrid, atrocious, and afflicting spectacle,* that perhaps was ever exhibited to the *pity* and *indignation* of mankind." That Mr. Burke's imagination was greatly affected by a scene, which he describes in the highest glow of colouring, I can well believe; but Dr. Price, who classes with that description of men stiled by Mr. Burke *abstract philosophers,* has been used to carry his mind, in a long series of ideas, to the consequences of actions which arise in the passing scene. Dr. Price then, with *full as much sympathy* in him *as even Mr. Burke* can have, might not be greatly moved with the mortifications and sufferings of a *very few*

few perfons, however highly diftinguifhed for the fplendour of their rank, when thofe mortifications led the way, or fecured the *prefent and future happinefs of twenty-four millions of people, with their pofterity*, emancipated by their *manly* exertions, from all that is *degrading* and *afflicting* to the fenfible mind; and let into the immediate bleffings of *perfonal fecurity*, and to the enjoyment of thofe advantages which above *all others* muft be delightful to the feelings of an high-fpirited people.

The *events* of human life, when *properly* confidered, are but a feries of *benevolent providences:* many of them, though very important in their confequences, are too much confounded with the common tranfactions of men, to be obferved; but whenever the believer thinks he perceives the *omnipotent will* more immediately declaring itfelf in favour of the future *perfection* and *happinefs* of the moral world, he is naturally led into the fame extafies of *hope* and *gratitude*, with which Simeon was tranfported by the view of the infant Meffiah. Has Mr. Burke never heard of any millenium, but that fanciful one which

is

is fuppofed to exift in the kingdom of the faints? If this fhould be the cafe, I would recommend to him to read *Newton on the prophecies.* He will find that this moft refpectable Bifhop, *who was no ranter*, is of opinion, that *fome paffages* in the Revelations point out a period of time when the *iron* fceptre of *arbitrary* fway fhall be broken; when *righteoufnefs fhall prevail* over the whole earth, and a *correct* fyftem of equity take place in the conduct of man. Every providence, therefore, by which any *infuperable object* to this tranfcendent bleffing appears to be taken away, muft rationally draw forth ejaculations of *gratitude* from the *benevolent* Chriftian. What ideas do more naturally affociate in the human mind, than thofe of the firft appearance of the infant Jefus, and his future univerfal reign in the hearts of his people?

But Mr. Burke thinks, that there was at leaft a great impropriety in expreffing an approbation of the fpirited conduct of the French nation, before time and circumftances had manifefted that the freedom they had gained, had been ufed with *wifdom* in the

D forming

forming a new conſtitution of government, or in improving the old one. "When I ſee," ſays Mr. Burke, " the ſpirit of liberty in action, I ſee a ſtrong principle at work; and this for a while is all I can poſſibly know of it. The wild gas, the fixed air is plainly broke looſe; but we ought to ſuſpend our judgment until the firſt effervescence is a little ſubſided, till the liquor is cleared, and until we ſee ſomething deeper than the agitation of a troubled and frothy ſurface."

The French Revolution was attended with ſomething ſo *new* in the hiſtory of human affairs; there was ſomething ſo *ſingular*, ſo *unique*, in that *perfect* unanimity in the people; in that *firm* ſpirit which baffled *every hope* in the *intereſted*, that they could poſſibly divide them into parties, and render them the inſtruments of a re-ſubjection to their old bondage; that it naturally excited the *ſurprize* and the *admiration* of all men. It appeared as a *ſudden ſpread of an enlightened ſpirit*, which promiſed to act as an effectual and permanent barrier to the inlet of thoſe uſurpations which from the very beginning of ſocial life the *crafty* have impoſed on *ignorance.*

This

This was a triumph of *sufficient importance* to call forth the exultation of individuals, and the approbation of focieties. But the two clubs who have the *misfortune* to fall under Mr. Burke's fevere cenfure, did not teftify a formal approbation of the conduct of their neighbours, till the deputies they had chofen for the tranfaction of their affairs, had manifefted a virtue *equal* to fo high a truft; for no fooner was the power of the court *fufficiently* fubdued to enable them to act with *freedom* and *effect*, than they gave an example of *difinterefted magnanimity*, that has *no parallel* in the conduct of *any* preceding affembly of men, and which was *never furpaffed by any individual*. That memorable day in which the members of the National Affembly, with a *virtuous enthufiafm*, vied with each other in the alacrity with which they furrendered to the people all their feudal privileges, will for ever ftand in the records of time as a monument of their *fingular greatnefs*. Such an inftance of human virtue was furely a *proper fubject of applaufe and congratulation*.

Men who have fuffered in their perfonal interefts by the new order of things in

France,

France, muſt naturally be inclined to *exaggerate* every blemiſh which appears in the conduct of a multitude, by whoſe ſpirit they have been deprived of many fond privileges. Their *petulant* obſervations, whilſt their minds are *heated* by imaginary wrongs and injuries, is *excuſable;* becauſe it is a *weakneſs* almoſt inſeparable from *human frailty.* It would, however, have become *Engliſhmen,* from whom might have been expected a *more ſympathiſing* indulgence towards the *friends* and *promoters* of liberty, to have been more *candid* in their cenſures; but in no part of Europe perhaps, have the evils which muſt *neceſſarily* attend all Revolutions, and eſpecially a Revolution ſo *complete* and *comprehenſive* as that which has taken place in France, been *more exaggerated,* and *more affectedly* lamented.

Had this *great work* been effected without the ſhedding one drop of *innocent* or even *guilty* blood, without doubt it would have better pleaſed the *generous* and *benevolent* mind. But, was it *poſſible* that ſuch a pleaſing circumſtance could ever have had an exiſtence? If we take into conſideration that *animofity* which fubfifted between the *arifto-cratifts* and *democratifts* on the eve of the Revolution, an animofity which was greatly heightened by the imprudent *infults* which the *Tier Etat* had received from the firft mentioned body, we fhall rather *wonder at the moderation* with which the people ufed their *complete* victory, than lament their cruelty. After the fuccefsful ftorming the king's camp, and the flight or defertion of his Janizaries, inftead of that *order* and voluntary *fubjection* to difcipline which appeared in an armed mob, and which prevented *all* infringement on the rights of property, had the fubdued party been delivered over to the *outrage* and the *pillage* of the rabble, the *horrid* fcene might have been *parallelled* by examples drawn from the guilty violence of *civilized* nations, without calling our attention to *Theban* and *Thracian orgies*, or a proceffion of American *favages* entering into *Onondaga*. I do not indeed exactly know how much blood has been fpilled in France, or how many individuals have fallen a facrifice in the public commotions; but by all the general accounts which have been tranfmitted to us, the hiftory of

monarchies

monarchies will point out as many fufferers who have fallen in *one hour* to the *rage* and *outrageous pride* of kingly defpots.

The punifhment of the lamp-poft, it muft be owned, ftrikes terror to the mind, and calls forth an immediate effufion of *fympathy* to the fufferer. But when *candid reflection* fuperfedes the *firft emotions* of human tender-nefs, this truth will force itfelf on our con-fideration, that a people who had been ufed to fuch *barbarous* fpectacles as that of behold-ing wretches, whofe *deftitute poverty* had in a manner *compelled* to the forlorn courfe of highway robbery, broken on a wheel, and *lingering* out the laft hours of life under the *agonifing* ftrokes of a ftern executioner, would naturally regard hanging as a *mild* punifh-ment on men whom they confidered as the worft of criminals. Let us rejoice, then, that fuch *dreadful legal executions*, which muft from their nature tend to *barbarize* men, are happily put an end to by the Revolu-tion.

But Mr. Burke is now come to a fcene which is calculated to draw forth *all* the ener-gies of his imagination, and which confe-

I

quently

quently he defcribes with the *higheft poffible* colouring. This is no other than the 6th of October 1789, when the king and queen were led in triumph to Paris. I very much *honour the king of France* for that eafe of temper which has enabled him to go through all his perfonal mortifications with a *manly dignity;* but it muft be confeffed that he brought them on himfelf, by a conduct, which, to fay the beft of it, was altogether imprudent.

The firft involuntary vifit which he made to the capital, was abfolutely neceffary, to appeafe the *fears* and the *refentment* which had been raifed by his *ineffectual* attempt to *awe* the deliberations and the refolutions of the National Affembly by an *armed force.* In the fecond, he was carried to Paris to *prevent* the execution of *a defign* formed by the court cabal, which, had it fucceeded, might have *deluged* the nation in blood, and furnifhed the fuel of civil difcord for years.

The Parifians fhewed no intention, or even defire, to deprive in any refpect their king of his perfonal liberty; till, by a very fufpicious conduct, he appeared to have mani-

feſted

fefted a defign to corrupt the fidelity of his guards to their new government, and to fet up the ftandard of arms in that quarter of the kingdom where the friends of defpotifm from every part of Europe might repair with fafety. The *great* and *unabating* rage and indignation which the enemies to the new conftitution have fhewn for what they term the captivity of the king, plainly evinces the *neceffity* that urged the meafure.

Having endeavoured to fhew the futility of Mr. Burke's obfervations and cenfures on the Revolution and Conftitutional Societies; and likewife, that his fevere pointed reflections on the conduct of the French nation, for having, as he fays, committed on the vanquifhed party the moft *unexampled* acts of atrocious violence, are not founded either in *truth* or *reafon;* I fhall proceed with my critical reflections on the animadverfions of my author, who goes on in a very *free manner* to cenfure every part of the French conftitution, to draw a comparifon between the Britifh and the Gallic governments as they now exift, and to eftablifh, in the way of reafoning,

reafoning, a fuperiority in favour of the government of his own country.

To fhew that the National Affembly have
committed a very *grofs* and *ruinous* error, in
the building a new ftructure, inftead of improving an old one ; Mr. Burke cites, in a
triumphant manner, the conduct of the Englifh nation. Our oldeft reformation, he obferves, is that of *Magna Charta.* " You will
fee, fays he, addreffing his correfpondent, that
Sir Edward Coke, that great oracle of our
law, and indeed all the great men who follow him to Blackftone, are induftrious to
prove the pedigree of our liberties. They
endeavour to prove, that the ancient Charta,
the Magna Charta of king John, was con-
nected with another pofitive Charta from
Henry the firft, and that both the one and
the other were nothing more than a re-affir-
mance of the ftill more ancient ftanding law
of the kingdom." " In the famous law of
the third of Charles the firft, called the Petition of Right, the Parliament fays to the king,
Your fubjects have inherited this freedom
(claiming their franchifes) not on abftract
principles as the rights of men, but as the

rights of Englishmen, and as a patrimony derived from their forefathers."

This language of the parliament, when pleading for the freedom of their countrymen at the tribunal of a prince's throne, who was as little inclined to *admit*, and whose *prejudices* enabled him as little to *understand* the only reasonable grounds of the argument as any despot who ever swayed an eastern sceptre, was well adapted to the *character* of the prince, and the *ignorance* of the multitude. But had the *circumstances* of Charles enabled him to *speak* and to *enforce* the sentiments of his mind, he would undoubtedly have made the following reply : You tell me upon your *own* authority, and the authority of *your lawyers*, that what you plead so strenuously for, is a patrimony derived from your forefathers, and grounded on the ancient law of the land. Be it so—Was not this ancient law *superseded by the authority of arms*, and the *entire* submission of the people to the Norman code established by William the Conqueror ? *Magna Charta*, then, and the other charters, must either have been *extorted* from the *imbecillity* of the princes who granted them,

them, or they muſt have iſſued from the *voluntary donations of monarchs;* in either caſe, they only ſtand on a *reſumable* right.

What the parliament could have anſwered to this plea, I know not, without calling in the aid of an *abſtract right;* which they endeavoured to keep out of the view of the king, with as much care as Mr. Burke *endeavours* to keep it out of the view of all men. But certain it is, that the king, though he did not explicitly declare with all their force the above mentioned ſentiments, yet he acted agreeable to their tenor the moment he got rid of this troubleſome aſſembly: For, conſidering the articles of the petition of right as a *gift depending on his pleaſure to fulfil or to reſume,* he broke them whenever they thwarted his ſyſtem of adminiſtration, and *impriſoned* thoſe who on the ſtrength of this ſtatute withſtood his authority.

I have myſelf always conſidered the boaſted birthright of an Engliſhman, as an *arrogant* pretenſion, built on a *beggarly* foundation. It is an arrogant pretenſion, becauſe it intimates a kind of excluſion to the reſt of mankind from the ſame privileges; and it is

E 2　　　　beggarly,

beggarly, becaufe it refts our legitimate freedom on the *alms* of our princes.

I muft own I was fomewhat furprifed to
find a gentleman of polifhed manners, who
has fpent the beft part of his life in the com-
pany of thofe who *affect* the niceft con-
formity to the rules of a refined civility,
addreffing the auguft reprefentatives of the
moft *gallant* and *refpectable* of the European
nations, in terms which I fhould not ufe to
a fet of chimney-fweepers, though acting the
moft ridiculoufly out of their fphere. Neither
do I chufe to repeat all thofe expreffions of
ineffable contempt, which the ftrong glow
of Mr. Burke's imagination has fcattered
through the whole of his reprehenfions.

It is not my intention to make any formal
comparifon between the new conftitution of
France, and the prefent exifting .conftitution
of England; or to prefume to cenfure a
government, from which an induftrious people receive protection, and with which the
large majority of the nation are entirely
fatisfied. Yet it may not be inexpedient to
obferve, that we cannot with any grounds
of *reafon* or *propriety*, fet up our own confti-

3   tution

tution as the model which all other nations ought *implicitly* to follow, unlefs we are *certain* that it beftows the *greateft* poffible happinefs on the people which in the nature of things any government can beftow. We ought to be *certain*, that this *model* will bear the moft *nice* and *critical* examination. It ought to be void of any of thofe *obvious*, or more *concealed* caufes, which produce *prefent evils*, and carry the mind to apprehenfions of *future mifchiefs*. We ought not at leaft to have had a *national debt*, fwelled to a *magnitude* which *terrifies* even the *moft fanguine* for its confequences. Our parliaments ought to have been *eminently* diftinguifhed for their *integrity*, and a *total* independence of any *corrupt influence;* and no *neceffity ought to have exifted in our affairs*, which have obliged us to *endure impofts* which our anceftors would have *rejected with horror*, and *refifted*. If an Englifhman fees any thing which is amifs in his own government, he ought not undoubtedly to look forward to any other remedy than thofe which the lenient hand of reformation will fupply. But when the old veffel of a common-wealth is *torn to pieces* by the

fhocks

fhocks it has fuftained from *contending parties ;* when the people, difdaining and rejecting all thofe fond opinions by which they have been *enflaved to mifery,* affert their native right of forming a government for themfelves; furely in fuch a cafe the builders are bound by no law of *duty* or *reafon* to make ufe of thefe old materials in the ftructure of their new conftitution, which they fuppofe to have been of an injurious tendency. The leaders of the French Revolution, and their followers, fee *none of thofe ftriking beauties* in the old laws and rules of the Gothic inftitutions of Europe, which Mr. Burke does. They do not profefs to have any of the fpirit of antiquarians among them; and they have not perceived, in the experience of old or ancient times, a *perfect harmony* arifing from *oppofition* of interefts; nor can they *underftand* how fuch a combination can be formed as fhall produce it. In fuch a view of things, they have chofen a fimple rule for the model of their new ftructure, yet regulated with all that *art* and *defign* which the experience of ages affords to the wifdom of man. They are accufed of having entirely difmiffed that ufeful guide *experience*

from

from their councils, but they think they have made *the beſt uſe* of it; whether this opinion of theirs is founded in truth, time, and the future hiſtory of man, muſt evince.

Mr. Burke, reaſoning from what I regard as a groundleſs ſuppoſition, very pathetically laments, and very ſeverely reprehends the conduct of thoſe, who, holding out falſe and treacherous lures to the king, led him into conceſſions fatal to his perſonal power, and the conſtitution of the monarchy. That the parliaments of France never intended to make any *alteration* in the old government, I am thoroughly perſuaded; and I am equally perſuaded, that they fondly imagined the people would *freely* give their money for the redreſs of ſome of the moſt heavy of the grievances under which they laboured. They knew, by the experience of paſt times, that in voting by orders, the people had never gained any *ſolid* advantage from an aſſembly of the States General. Neither the court, nor the parliament of Paris, who made the king ſo many ſplendid promiſes, were aware of the conſequences. which muſt ariſe from the general ſpread of knowledge among the people;
and

and in the event of things, they were *both dif-appointed* of their purpofes ; for the *Tier Etat*, reflecting on the *old practices* which the *crown*, the *clergy*, and the *nobility* had ufed againft them, were determined to throw the whole weight of their natural fcale into the balance, and to redrefs their own grievances, without waiting the effect of *humble* petitions and *difcordant* councils. That neither the king, nor the parliaments of France, could long have prevented the *full* exertion of this power, (had they forefeen all the confequences which did arife from fuffering the meeting of the States General), is to me very plain. A *regeneration* of the conftitution would have been *equally* effected ; but it would have been attended with a *tremendous* difference in its circumftances. It would have been ufhered in by a general bankruptcy, and the wafte of civil blood. " Our enemies," fays a popular Leader in the National Affembly, " may, by their machinations, make us buy our liberties dear, but they cannot deprive us of them." " This breach of confidence," as Mr. Burke terms it, " to an eafy and condefcending king, will have a

dreadful

dreadful effect on the interests of mankind, by sanctifying the dark suspicious maxims of tyrannous distrust; and will teach kings to tremble at what will be called the delusive plausibilities of *moral politicians.*" Be this as it may, the people of France had *certainly* a right to provide for their own *security* and *welfare* on those principles which *they* thought the most conducive to this *great end*, and to leave it to the wisdom of other nations to make suitable provision for theirs. It behoves them, however, to be careful to *cherish* and *preserve* the liberty they have *so nobly* gained; to suffer no intemperate spirit to produce that licentiousness which must bring anarchy in its train; nor to indulge a *capricious impatience*, by which their enemies, in working on their passions and *misguiding* their reason, may reduce them to their old state of bondage; in which case it is *certain*, power will reap *many* advantages from past transactions, by which it will be enabled to *tie fast* those *fetters* the giddy people will so well deserve.

Though I have hitherto spared my readers a detail of all the severe invectives which Mr. Burke has used against the leading mem-

F

bers who compofe the National Affembly;
yet, for the fake of thofe principles of *moral
rectitude* which the torrent of his eloquence
appears to *baffle* and *confound*, it will be neceffary to notice his obfervations on the character and conduct of the nobles who have
taken the lead in the French revolution, and
who yet continue to fupport it. He accufes
them with having affifted in the fpoil and
humiliation of their own order, to poffefs a
fure fund for their new followers. " To be
attached to the fubdivifion, to love the little
platoon we belong to in fociety (fays Mr.
Burke) is the firft principle, the germ as it
were, of public affections : it is the firft link
in the feries by which we proceed towards a
love of our country and mankind."

What *fplendid emoluments* and what *grand
objects* of perfonal ambition thofe noblemen
could have in view, who, whilft they *gene-
roufly* facrificed thofe privileges which are the
moft fondly coveted by human vanity, fhut
out their entrance to the public offices of the
ftate, by refolutions which rendered fuch pro-
motions incompatible with their legiflative
truft, I know not; but I hope we fhall not

be

be fo much *blinded* with the fplendour of dazzling images, as to confound thofe *narrow affections* which bind fmall bodies together by the mutual ties of perfonal intereft, to that *liberal benevolence*, which, difdaining the confideration of every felfifh good, chearfully facrifices *a perfonal intereft* to the *welfare* of the community.

Of the lift of individuals whom Mr. Burke felects as examples of *true glory*, and as benefactors rather than deftroyers of their country, fome of them ought to have been for ever ftampt with *infamy*, as the *pefts* and *tyrants* of their fpecies; and they are all of them of doubtful fame, as to any *honour* derived to their country by their ambitious projects, unlefs a *nation of flaves can receive glory* from *a capacity* of becoming the *fcourge* of other focieties.

Richlieu was the grand inftrument by which the court of France, in the reign of Louis the fourteenth, was enabled to maffacre the greater part of the French Hugonots, and to drive the remainder out of the kingdom. Cromwell, indeed, who deprived his fovereign of life, *merely to ufurp his power*, has, with many people, paid the debt of his crimes, by having,

through

through the general deteftation which men conceived of his *treachery* and *tyranny*, rendered the Revolution and the Revolutionifts odious, and thus paved the way for the reftoration of the old government.

In the next argument prefented to our attention, Mr. Burke has very ftrongly entrenched himfelf in the holds of the Britifh conftitution; and we will not attempt to purfue him into his fortrefs: For, though a natural vanity *might flatter us* with a *delufive hope* of victory, arifing from the fubtle objections which may be urged to every political propofition; yet the victory would coft *too dear*, if it fubjected us to the reproach of any defign againft the peace and quiet of the community. But it will not, I think, be deviating from the higheft point of decency and prudence, to make our objections to his general affertions. His propofition, " that it is the great maffes of property which form a natural rampart about the leffer properties in all their gradations," is not in our opinion founded in truth; for every citizen who poffeffes ever fo *fmall* a fhare of property, is *equally* as tenacious of it as the moft opulent member

member of fociety ; and this leads him to *refpect* and to *fupport* all the laws by which property is protected. It is this fenfe of perfonal intereft, which, running through every rank in fociety, and attaching itfelf to every one of its members who are not in the condition of a pauper, forms an impenetrable barrier to the fecurity of wealth ; for otherwife, as the numbers of the opulent muft be *very* fmall in proportion to the number of thofe who form the great mafs of the people, *envy* would operate fo fuccefsfully againft them as to deftroy the force of artificial fupports.

When the conftitution of France is compleatly fettled, and the commonwealth refts upon its bafis, this difpofition of the human mind, which operates fo powerfully for the prefervation of peace and order, will, as on former occafions, regain its natural force. For the operations of *power* on the property of the citizen, is not an *unexampled* event in the hiftories of civil focieties.

The manner in which the National Affembly of France have endeavoured to fecure and to defend the liberty of the different towns and provinces which compofe that vaft empire, come next under Mr. Burke's fevere criticifm.

criticifm. But in his *endeavour* to bring.men
over to his fentiments on this fubject, he is
obliged to have recourfe to all thofe *unfair*
means which perfons of genius think themfelves entitled to ufe in the courfe of their
argument; for what, indeed, but the *delufive*
power of a fubtle fophiftry, can produce an
apparent *concord* between propofitions the
moft *oppofite in their nature?* and what but
an appeal to the paffions of the reader, can
prevent his affent to the *moft obvious truths?*

The National Affembly of France are at
one time accufed by Mr. Burke of a fcheme
for *perpetuating* their power, at the expence
of the rights of election; at another, of acting
weakly and *meanly* in the having *limited* their
fitting to the *fhort fpace of two years.* In one
view of things, they are accufed of drawing
to themfelves, and to the city of Paris, *an ex-*
orbitance of power, which, if not refifted, muft
end in the total fubjection of the provinces,
whofe natural productions and acquired
wealth are to be exhaufted to pamper the
luxury and gratify the avarice of the capital.
In another, their politics are arraigned, for having left no leading *controuling power* in the
empire, of *fufficient energy* to fupport a necef-

fary

fary fubordination of its parts. Such *palpable contradictions*, fuch *little arts* of *mifreprefentation* we have feen daily thrown out in the public papers by the *hoftile faction*, who naturally endeavour to *miflead* the people into a *diftruft* of their deputies, becaufe they have guarded their liberties with too nice and too jealous a care. But we did not expect to fee them collected together and fet off with all the powers of literary compofition, by one of the greateft orators of the age; and this in a work which the author holds out as an *exact ftandard*, by which the limits of *power* and of *freedom* are from henceforth *to receive their bounds*. Neither did we expect to find that the *humane* writer would have fo far entered into the paffions of the difcontented party, as to *envy* the people of Paris that bread which is fo neceffary for their fubfiftence, and which cannot be otherwife fupplied but by the produce of the provinces.

We were alfo greatly furprized to find Mr. Burke entering into fuch contradictions, as at *one time* to reprefent the excellencies of the Englifh conftitution as *obvious* to every obferver, and fo fenfibly felt by its fubjects as *unanimoufly* to bind their affections to its

principles,

principles, its rules, and its dictates ; to the
exception only of a few *idle, insignificant,
speculative individuals:* and *at another, trem-
bling* left if the queftion of the abftract rights
of men were brought before the eyes of the
people, the moft *dreadful* confufions might
follow, and be attended with the *utter down-
fall* of every order in the church and ftate,
of *every exclusive* privilege exifting in its
bodies corporate, and with the *general* pillage of the rich.

Such reprefentations are certainly well
adapted to *rouse* the felfifh paffions of the
timid mind, and may ferve the prefent purpofe of the *hour ;* but they will not ftand the
more *candid* and *cool* decifions which attend
on *time.*

The *legitimate* power by which governments are made or altered, muft either ftand
on the *native rights* of the fpecies, or it muft
ftand on an authority vefted in an individual,
or in a limited number of individuals, ex-
alted to this authority, either by the pofitive
law of a *revealed will,* or by fome native fuperiority *evidently* attached to their perfons.
That this facred truft has never been fo for-
mally

mally vested in *any* individual, or in *any given number* of individuals, is in a manner acknowledged by the moſt ſtrenuous advocates for *paſſive obedience;* for all their arguments are built on preſumptive grounds.

The contrary propoſition to this, *viz. that native right in the ſocial body to chooſe its own government,* which Mr. Burke *condemns* under the deſcription of a *metaphyſical foolery,* is allowed with all its weight of authority by the greateſt part of the Engliſh Revolutioniſts; nor can any other *reaſonable* ground of perſuaſion be made uſe of, to bring the people to concur in any plan of ſalutary or neceſſary reformation. With what pretence then, can Mr. Burke charge Dr. Price, or any of his adherents or admirers, with advancing a *novel* or a *miſchievous* doctrine, when they aſſert that all legitimate power is founded on the rights of nature? " But government (ſays Mr. Burke) is not made in virtue of natural rights, which may and do exiſt in total independence of it; and exiſt in much greater clearneſs, and in a much greater degree of abſtract perfection; but their abſtract perfection is their practical de-

G   fect.

fect. By having a right to every thing, they want every thing. Government is a contrivance of human wifdom, to provide for human wants. Men have a right that thefe wants fhould be provided for by this wifdom. Among thefe wants is to be reckoned the want out of a civil fociety, of a fufficient reftraint upon their paffions. Society requires not only that the paffions of individuals fhould be fubjected, but even in the mafs and body, as well as in the individuals; the inclinations of men fhould frequently be thwarted, their will controuled, and their paffions brought into fubjection. This can only be done by a power out of themfelves, and not in the exercife of its functions, fubject to that will, and to thofe paffions, which it is in its office to bridle and fubdue. In this fenfe, the reftraints of men, as well as their liberties, are to be reckoned among their rights."

To this very *ingenious* reafoning, and thefe *refined* diftinctions between natural and focial rights, the people may poffibly object, that in delivering themfelves *paffively* over to the *unreftrained rule of others*, on the plea of controul-

ing

ing *their inordinate inclinations* and *paſſions,*
they deliver themſelves over to *men,* who, as
men, and partaking of the *ſame* nature as
themſelves, are as liable to be governed by
the ſame *principles* and *errors;* and to men
who, by the great ſuperiority of their ſtation,
having no *common* intereſt with themſelves
which might lead them to preſerve a ſalutary
check over their vices, muſt be inclined to
abuſe in the *groſſeſt manner* their truſt. To
proceed with Mr. Burke's argument, ſhould
the rich and opulent in the nation plead
their right to the predominant fway in ſociety, from its being a neceſſary circumſtance
to guard their wealth from the gripe of poverty, the men in an inferior ſtate of fortune might argue, that ſhould they give way
to this plea in all its extent, their moderate
poſſeſſions would be expoſed to the burden of
unequal taxes; for the rich, when poſſeſſed
of the *whole* authority of the ſtate, would be
ſure to take the *firſt care* of themſelves, if
they ſhould not be tempted to ſecure an ex-
oneration of *all* burthens, by dividing the
ſpoils of the public; and that the *abuſe* of
ſuch high truſts muſt *neceſſarily* ariſe, be-

cauſe

caufe to act by felfifh confiderations, is in the very conftitution of our nature.

To fuch pleas, fo plaufibly urged on all fides, I know of no *rational* objection; nor can I think of any expedient to remove the well-grounded apprehenfions of the different interefts which compofe a commonwealth, than a *fair* and *equal* reprefentation of the *whole* people;—a circumftance which appears very peculiarly neceffary in a mixed form of government, where the democratic part of the conftitution will ever be in danger of being overborne by the energy attending on its higher conftituent parts.

On fuch grounds of reafoning, there will be found no infuperable objections to thofe propofitions of Dr. Price, which are fo highly cenfured by Mr. Burke, as containing principles of the moft *feditious* and *dangerous* nature; even though we fhould allow that every government which accords with the opinions and the inclinations of the large majority of the people, is, in an high fenfe of the term, a legitimate government.

We fhall now proceed with that courfe of the argument in which Mr. Burke endea-

vours

vours to fhew, that the *unequal* reprefentation which he allows to have taken place in *our government*, is a *perfection* rather than a *defect*. " With us, when we elect popular reprefen- tatives, (fays Mr. Burke, ftill addreffing his French correfpondent), we fend them to a council in which each man individually is a fubject, and fubmitted to a government com- plete in all its ordinary functions. With you the elective affembly is the fovereign, and the fole fovereign; all the members therefore are integral parts of this fole fovereignty. But with us, it is totally different. With us, the reprefentatives feparated from the other parts, can have no action, and no ex- iftence. The government is the point of re- ference of the feveral members and diftricts of our reprefentation. This is the centre of our unity. This government of reference is a truftee for the whole, and not for the parts. So is the other branch of our public council; I mean the Houfe of Lords. With us, the King and the Lords are feveral and joint fe- curities for the equality of each diftrict, each province, each city. When did you hear in Great Britain, of any province fuffering from

the

the inequality of reprefentation? what diftrict from having no reprefentation at all?
Not only our monarchy and our peerage fecure the equality on which our unity depends, but it is the fpirit of the Houfe of
Commons itfelf. The very inequality of reprefentation, which is fo *foolifhly* complained
of, is perhaps the very thing which prevents
us from thinking or acting as members for
diftricts. Cornwall elects as many members
as all Scotland; but is Cornwall better taken
care of than Scotland?"

If your Lordfhip fees the refult of this argument in the fame light as I do, you will
confider it as equally recommendatory to an
election of the *Lower Houfe* in the *King* and
the *Lords*, as of an inadequate reprefentation
made by the election of the Commons. For
if the *King* and the *Lords* are feveral and
joint fecurities for the equality of each diftrict, each province, and each city; why
fhould we throw the country into a ftate of
riot and *confufion* every feven years? Why
fhould we put ourfelves to electioneering *ex-*
pences? Would it not be a *more convenient*
method

method to fuffer the *King* and the Houfe of *Lords to chufe* our reprefentatives?

But this is not the point of view in which the friends of equal reprefentation fee the neceffity of a reform: they do not alledge that Cornwall is better taken care of than any other diftrict in Great Britain. The fubject of their complaint is, that the important interefts of the great body of the Commons is, by our *prefent inadequate ftate of reprefentation*, facrificed to the ambition of *private* individuals, who, by their *command* over boroughs, may make their *market* with government at the *expence* of the public. The *ftrong* and *firm* oppofition which the *ruling powers* have given to *every* ftep towards this *reafonable* reformation, is not *one* of the *happieft* effects which arife from that continual war of *interefts* fo much admired by Mr. Burke and others. The jealoufy it manifefts of the people, is without *all* bounds of moderation; for the organ by which the democratic influence is exerted, has no very formidable energy. Its power is circumfcribed and fhut in by the immoveable barrier of laws, ufages, pofitive rules of doctrine

and

and practice, counterpoifed by the Houfe of Lords, and in a manner *fubjected to the Crown* by the prerogative of calling and diffolving parliaments.

To proceed with the obfervations of my author—After a torrent of the moft pointed invective, Mr. Burke takes upon him to cenfure every part of the conduct of the French Revolutionifts ; and among other acts, *one* which I have always confidered as founded in *truth, religion,* and the *pureft morality;* it is that of annihilating, by the force of a bright example, thofe notions founded on *falfe* principles of honour, which fell fo *feverely* and fo *cruelly* on every family who had the misfortune to have produced one *real* or *pretended* culprit. The infamy which families fuftained for the mifconduct of any of its individual members, was one of the *ftrongeft* reafons which have been urged for *perfonal* imprifonment at pleafure ; and when this dreadful engine of defpotifm was removed, it furely became expedient to *emancipate* the people from the *terror* of this impending evil. But when the *moft laudable tranfactions* of men are reprefented as *crimes,* we ought to be *cautious* how

how we give ear to the fuggeftions of their
accufer.

In the perfonal mortifications of the Queen
of France, Mr. Burke finds great reafon to
lament that the age of chivalry is no more;
for, had the fame fpirit exifted in this, that
exifted in paft ages, " ten thoufand fwords
might have leaped from their fcabbards, to
avenge even a look that threatened her with
infult." The high colouring given by Mr.
Burke to thofe fcenes of regal diftrefs, will, I
doubt not, captivate the imagination of the
greater number of his readers, in a degree
equal to the effects produced on the author
by the *charms* of the Queen of France. But
the *delufions* of fancy are apt to fubfide in
men of *cool* minds, when any *great* object of
public concern is held up to their view, to
the prejudice even of beauty and dignity,
and all thofe external objects, adapted rather
to *enflave* our affections, than to *lead* our
judgment.

The bringing the king and queen to Paris, and thus, by preventing their efcape, to
difable them from forming new troubles in
the kingdom, was certainly regarded as a

meafure

meafure of the *higheſt neceſſity;* and in this view, muſt have been approved by the true friends of the revolution, although it was attended with tumult and diſorder.

The age in which the ſpirit of chivalry was triumphantly prevalent, would indeed have been a very *improper* time to have attempted a regeneration of conſtitutions on a *popular* principle ; but I have always regarded the neceſſity which gave birth to the orders of chivalry, as a mark of *diſgrace* to the times in which they were formed. They were indeed a proper remedy to the evils ariſing from *ferocity, ſlavery, barbariſm,* and *ignorance ;* but now, when the cauſes no longer exiſt which rendered them uſeful, we ſhould rather think of *freeing* ſociety of all the evils inherent in thoſe *falſe* notions of honour which they have given riſe to, than endeavour to call back their ſpirit in its full force. That enthuſiaſtic military fire, that *methodized ſentimental barbariſm,* which inſtigates men to deprive their fellow-citizens of life for *ſuppoſed* perſonal affronts, in *defiance* of the laws of *religion* and *ſociety,* are the offsprings of chivalry, and unknown to *all*

the

the nations of the *ancient civilized* world. But it is the *simplicity* of all *abstract princi- ples*, against which Mr. Burke makes an *eternal* war; all the *devices* of pride, all the *fond conceits* of vanity, all the train of *pompous* ostentation, by which *naked* virtue is put *out* of her *rank*, to give way to the more imposing glare of external magnificence, are reprefented as useful ideas, " furnished from the wardrobe of a *moral* imagination, which the heart owns, and the underftanding ratifies, as necessary to cover the defects of our naked shivering nature, and to raife it to dignity in our own eftima- tion."

It is not, according to *these* ideas, recom- mended by Mr. Burke, that the Scripture teaches us to *respect ourselves*; and although the maxims of the facred writings are ex- ploded by all politicians as *incompatible* with their views, yet certainly the *excellency* of their precepts consists in their being *exactly* fitted to a *temporal* as well as to a *spiritual* happinefs. Neither in a *moral* view of things, can I perceive how the *ornaments* of artificial greatnefs, which is found to anfwer

H 2

all

all the purpofes of *human pride*, fhould affift
us in acquiring that *true* dignity of character which *alone* ought to conftitute diftinction; nor how we can truly refpect ourfelves, by *idolizing* the *mere phantom* of greatnefs, whether it be attached to our own perfons, or the perfons of others.

As every act of the French National Affembly is to be *condemned*, not only in the
grofs, but in the *detail*, the addrefs of congratulation to the king on the commencement
of the prefent year, comes, among others,
under Mr. Burke's fevere animadverfion.

I have not indeed got this addrefs by me;
but if my memory does not deceive me, it
contained a language the *beft* adapted to footh
the perfonal afflictions of the king. Not the
fmalleft hint was given, that any ill conduct
in his Majefty had provoked the people to
emancipate themfelves from his power; it
thanked him for his concurrence with their
wifhes; it reprefented their liberty as the
neceffary confequence of their *enlightened*
fpirit, not of their fufferings under his adminiftration; and it promifed as loyal an attachment to his perfon, and to the diftinction

he

he held as the firſt magiſtrate of the commonwealth, as could have been exacted by the
authority of which he was diſpoſſeſſed.

Whatever might have been held out as
the oſtenſible object of the people in their de-
mand for the meeting of their repreſenta-
tives, it certainly was intended by them to
uſe their power, when thus veſted with a
legitimate form, and endued with a capa-
bility of legiſlation, not only to the *reformation* of abuſes, but to the *regeneration* of
their conſtitution; and thus the National Aſſembly became veſted with the truſt of legiſlation, in the *higheſt* ſenſe of the word: nor
could this truſt be *limited* or *governed* by any
of thoſe rules and practices, which, for *rea-
ſons* drawn from *experience,* the people *condemned,* and were *determined to aboliſh.*

Thus the preſerving the ſtate from the
ruin of an impending bankruptcy, *brought
on* by the *prodigality* of courts, and the *regeneration* of the conſtitution, were the important ſervices which the National Aſſembly
were expected to perform for their conſtitu-
ents. And when we conſider that theſe *important* and *difficult* ſervices were to be per-
formed

formed without that ready and effectual in-
strument of power, a *standing* army, (in
whom *implicit* obedience is the *only* rule of
action), we shall be obliged to confess, either
that the men who undertook this *great* work
were infected with a *daring insanity*, or that
they were seconded by an *unanimity* in the
sentiments of the people, which is *unparal-
leled* in the history of large empires, and
which evidently destroys the force of *every*
accusation which can be brought against
them, as having rendered themselves the *in-
strument* of a faction, rather than the *faithful*
deputies of the people.

A total reformation [in the ecclesiastical
system, and the new modelling the system of
jurisprudence, were the *two leading points* in
which *every* member of the empire agreed,
excepting those individuals whose interests
were personally affected by a change. It was
a point of union in which both the nobility and the people met ; and several of those
persons who have been the *loudest* in their
exclamations against the conduct of the National Assembly, for having *disappointed* their
body of the largest share of the *spoils of the
crown*,

crown, and who have fince united themfelves to the *mal-contents* among the lawyers and the clergy, were the moft active in the firft movements of thefe grand points of reformation.

To begin with the reformation of the ecclefiaftical fyftem—It was thought by the French nation, that *one hundred and four fcore* millions of property, principally confined to the ufe of the *higher* orders of the clergy, and thus prevented from entering into the common circulation of other parts of property, was a *nuifance* in a treble fenfe. It was a *nuifance*, in the firft inftance, as a monopoly; in the fecond, it was a nuifance, as giving a dangerous power to thofe who poffeffed that monopoly; and in the third inftance, as it tended, by the *natural courfe* of moral caufes in this *its excefs*, to *corrupt* rather than to *encreafe* and *invigorate* thofe *qualities of the mind*, and thofe *fpiritual endowments*, which are to be defired in the teachers of religion. What real grounds there were for this opinion, fo generally conceived by the French nation in the conduct of the clergy, I know not; neither fhall I enquire,

quire,

quire, for *I am as little* inclined as Mr. Burke can be to infult the unfortunate: I fhall only fay, that as their temptations were *great*, and that their *nature* was not *fuperior* to human infirmity, it was *probable* they produced their *due* effects. But there is *one* fentiment in which I in fome meafure accord with Mr. Burke. I do moft fincerely lament that the *exigencies* of the times would *not fuffer* the National Affembly to indulge their clergy in a life-enjoyment of their poffeffions. But this fentiment of mine is not of *fo forcible* a kind as to deftroy *all other* fympathies. It would not lead me, even if I poffeffed a fimilar portion of abilities with Mr. Burke, like him, to *endeavour*, by the animating power of declamation, fo to condole with the fufferers as to combine all the energies of the *worft* paffions of men in favour of my opinion. I fhould not attempt to *roufe* and *inflame* the refentment of the French clergy to a *repetition* of acts which have renewed fcenes of violence, and by which, after the *manner of old times*, they have fet up the ftandard of Chrift crucified, *to arm bigotry* in favour of *their* pretenfions. Neither fhould I, among the more

peaceable

peaceable members of that body, by reprefentations the moft touchingly affecting, open
afrefh thofe wounds on which it is to be
hoped *religion has poured her healing balm.*

In the *attempt* to make the French National
Affembly *fingularly odious,* for the confifcations
they have made of the church-lands, Mr.
Burke afferts, that in many inftances they have
more violently outraged the principle, as well
as the forms of public juftice, than has been
done by any other preceding power. The
examples he brings in proof, are the confifcations made by the fury of triumphant fac-
tions in the Roman commonwealth; and an
example more in point in the perfon of Henry
the Eighth, for Mr. Burke does *not chufe* to
extend his obfervations to the conduct of
Denmark, Sweden, and other ftates, on their
profeffion of the reformed religion. Mr.
Burke confiders the *violences* of Marius and
Sylla to be *much graced* in the formalities of
falfe accufations of treafon againft the *moft virtuous perfons* in the commonwealth; and that
the tyrant Henry the Eighth, who feized the
property of the clergy for his own private
ufe, and the emoluments of his favourites,

I   *dignified*

dignified thefe aƈts of violence, by affuming the charaƈter of the judge, and condemning the viƈtims on *falfe pretences*. Surely the French clergy would not have thought themfelves *better ufed*, if the National Affembly had fet on foot a commiffion to examine into the crimes and abufes which prevailed among them, and then to have governed their proceedings by reported truths, mixed with exaggeration and falfehood; furely this *mockery* of juftice, *fo much ufed* in old times, and this *covering* to the *deeds* of power, by *fpoils torn* from the only confolatory remains of the fufferer, *his good fame*, will not be thought an example *proper* to have been followed, rather than the *plain* dealing of the French legiflature.

But Mr. Burke has as great a diflike to the reform of the church police, as to the confifcations of the property of the more dignified part of the order. He is quite in a *rage*, that the *poor curates* fhould be taken out of the *hopelefs poverty* into which they were plunged; and he *cannot endure* thofe regulations which took place in the *beſt* times of Chriftian focieties. That bifhops *ſhould be confined* to

their

their diocefes, and the *care* of their fpiritual
adminiftration, inftead of attending courts,
and lavifhing their incomes in the pleafures
of the capital; and that the people fhould
affume their rights of election; " are folecifms
in policy, which none but *barbarous, ignorant,
atheiftical minds* could dictate, and which no
man of *enlarged* capacity and *generous* paffions
can obey."

On that article of the French ecclefiaftical
policy which confines bifhops to their epif-
copal adminiftration, it may not be improper
to obferve, that Bifhop Leighton, the *moft
eminent* of the Scotch prelates for his *piety*
and his *zeal* for that order, *ardently wifhed*
that fuch a regulation fhould take place on
their re-eftablifhment in Scotland under
Charles the Second. I am far from faying
that fuch a regulation is compatible with the
ftate of things among us; and I think fo well
of the moderation of the clergy, and their
regard to the conftitution of the country, that
I wifh they were as *independent* a body as
Mr. Burke *reprefents them to be.* But furely
if *gratitude* for *paft favours,* the *hopes* held
out to *ambition* for the acquiring *further pre-*

I 2 *ferments,*

ferments, and a very confiderable number of church-livings in the *difpofal* of the crown, *can in any refpeɛt* influence the minds of the clergy, they cannot be faid to be *totally* independent.

I fhall now take into confideration the fecond grand point of reformation, in which the nobles and people appear at firft to have been in union, *viz.* the *new* modelling the fyftem of jurifprudence; but that a fyftem of jurifprudence, formed by *ignorant barbarians*, from codes of law adapted to fupport the *defpotic tyranny* of the *Roman Emperors*, could not be in unifon with the fentiments of an enlightened people, or capable of fupporting the principles of a *free* government, was apparent to all parties: but perfonal intereft, for reafons as apparent, at length produced an union between the lawyers and nobles. The National Affembly *juftly* thought, that laws dictated by the *humane* fpirit of an enlightened age, would be but *ill* adminiftered by a tribunal formed under the influence of the *rankeft* prejudices; and they conceived it as a *folecifm* in politics, that Parliaments, who had been efpecially appointed to fee that the laws and regulations framed by the Af-

femblies

femblies of the States General, fhould receive no injury from the edicts of the monarch, fhould be kept as a controul over the ftanding authority of the nation. It was on this reafon that the old independent Parliaments, with all their merits, and all their faults, were abolifhed. Nor is it a wonder that in the change of the *profpect*, a change in the *fenti-ments* of the nobles fhould have taken place: for when they perceived that the fyftem of the ancient tyranny was *better* adapted to their *perfonal* greatnefs than the *new order* of things, they, with Mr. Burke, looked on the Parliaments as a *convenient* power, under which they might rally. What a *ready convenience* for the play of a *delufive* policy would it have afforded, if the Parliaments, exerting their *old* authority under the crown, had pertinacioufly refufed to regifter the edicts of the Affembly! What a difplay of eloquence *in favour* of the *privileges* of the *nobles* and the *clergy*, might have been feen in their *remon-ftrances* to the Affembly! and what *ufeful* delays would it have afforded for the prefident of the National Affembly, in the name of the Majefty of the people, to have been obliged to

mount

mount the Bed of *Juſtice*, after the example
of the late monarchs of the realm; and in
caſe of an *incurable* obſtinacy, for the Aſſembly, through the means of the executive power,
to have recourſe to the *tedious* remedy of an
impriſonment. With ſuch advantages on their
ſide, the *faction* in oppoſition would have
had *reaſonable* grounds of hope, that *centuries*
might have elapſed before the conſtitution
could have been in any ſenſe of the word
regenerated.

Before I leave this ſubject, it will be neceſſary to notice, that Mr. Burke *condemns* the
conduct of the National Aſſembly for the
diſtinction they have made in their treatment
of the lawyers and their clergy, a diſtinction
which I think every unprejudiced perſon
will agree to be founded in juſtice, *viz.* the
preference afforded the former by making
them a ſuitable proviſion during life, in conſideration that the civil offices, of which
they were deprived, had been purchaſed with
private property (as Mr. Burke obſerves)
" at an high rate."

The prevention of a national bankruptcy
was thought an object of the moſt *momentous*

concern to the whole French nation. It was in order to avert this *impending* evil, that the States General were permitted to affemble; and it was an object *principally* recommended to the deputies of the people, by their united voice. In this ftate of public opinion, the arguments fo plaufibly, and indeed fo forcibly urged by Mr. Burke *againft the right* of the monarch to mortgage the public revenue, will not render the Affembly culpable for *endeavouring* to *keep faith* with the creditors of the crown. For though I never could perceive why on any *good grounds of reafon*, the people fhould *quarrel* with their new conftitution, becaufe the *prodigality* of the *old government* had involved them in *diftreffes* which were in their nature irremoveable, which did not proceed from any *fraud* or *corruption* in their *new* fervants, and which could not be mended by fubjecting themfelves to the *old* domination; yet certain it is, that the *enemies* of the new conftitution have beheld the arrival of a moment big with that temporary diftrefs and confufion which muft ever attend a national bankruptcy, with the *utmoft impatience*, as of bringing with it

4　　　　　　　　　　　a *fure*

a *sure* profpect of *victory*. What an *opportunity* indeed, would it prefent, of fetting
forth *exaggerated* defcriptions of public diftreffes, and of arraigning the members of
the National Affembly as the *fole* authors of
the nation's wrongs! The *anxious* and *provi-
dent* care which this Affembly has taken to
ward off this difafter, and alfo to avoid, in the
prefent irritable ftate of the public feelings,
the impofing very heavy burthens on the people, is certainly a mark of political *fagacity*,
and, *being fuch*, is treated with the *utmoft bit-
ternefs of difappointed rage* by their oppo-
nents.

On the fubject of the difficulties which the
French Legiflature have encountered in the
tafk of regenerating the conftitution, it is natural to turn our minds on the *paper-currency*
they have eftablifhed, and efpecially as it is
a fubject on which Mr. Burke has difplayed
the *whole force* of his ingenuity, to alarm the
fears of the French nation, and to depreciate,
and to render odious in their eyes, the conduct of their reprefentatives.

On this fubject I do profefs a total ignorance: I have no financiering abilities; and I
wifh

wiſh with all my heart, that this art which
Mr. Burke reprefents as a talent the *moſt
highly* neceffary in thofe who conduct the affairs of ftate, and which I confider as de-
riving its practical ufe from its *deceptious* addrefs in *picking the pockets* of the people, was
not fo neceffary an engine in the prefent
modes of adminiftration. A few obfervations
however, which muft occur to every thinking mind, I fhall venture to make. They are
as follows: That the difference which Mr.
Burke makes between the paper-currency of
this country, and that which now fubfifts in
France, is not *fo much* in favour of England
as Mr. Burke reprefents; for, as the French
legiflature have *not* iffued more paper than
they appear to have a *folid fund to fupport*,
and a fund that is *obvious* to every man's eyes
and underftanding, its credit *ought not in
reafon* to have lefs ftability than a paper cur-
rency founded on *confidence*. For, though
every man believes, and on good grounds believes, that the bank of England has a fufficient property to anfwer for the payment of
its notes; yet ftill although *this belief* fhould
arife to a *moral certainty*, it cannot be *fuperior*

K   to

to a credit founded on an *obvious* fact. And
fhould the French legiflature continue this
wife caution, of not iffuing more paper
than the ftate revenue can obvioufly fupport,
whilft the revolution ftands on its *prefent* bot-
tom, this paper, *whatever may be* the exigencies of the times, muft *always* be of *fome
value;* whereas a failure of our national credit would, it is generally thought, render the
paper money of this country of *no more worth
than the intrinfic value of the paper.*

The diffufion of a general fpirit of gaming,
and the deftructive practice of ftock-jobbing,
are evils which I am afraid in a more or
lefs degree muft ever exift with national debts;
and the *larger* the debt, the *greater* will be
the degree of evil. That this fpirit prevails
in our capital to a very alarming height, the
hiftory of the *Bulls* and *Bears* in the alley
will *abundantly* teftify: That it has been the
ruin of many a fair fortune, *thoufands of fufferers* can alfo teftify: That it has *enabled*
and *tempted feveral* of thofe who are in the
fecret of affairs, to *pillage* rhe public unmer-
cifully, fame reprefents; and that the ftocks
have a *great* influence over the landed pro-
I   perty

perty of this country, which rifes or falls according to their various fluctuations, the experience of the laft American war *evinces beyond a doubt.*

All thefe evils, if evils they are, were *prognofticated* by thofe who ftiled themfelves the patriots of their country, from the *firft* eftablifhment of a funded debt, to almoft the prefent period of time ; and the reafons they urged to enforce the arguments they ufed againft the meafure, appear to me fufficiently convincing to have induced a *cautious moderation* in our councils. But they were not attended to ; they were reprefented as the *chimeras of difcontented fpeculative men;* the *encreafe* of the national debt was fet forth as both the *caufe* and the *effects* of public *profperity;* it was defcribed as the *enlivening* principle of commerce, the *grand panacea* that was to keep us in an *eternal vigour,* the *fteady hold* by which all the members of the community were to be *bound* in the bands of loyalty ; and that there was *no excefs* in the amount of the debt, that could be attended with *any ruinous* confequences.

If

If fuch reprefentations, fo repeatedly made by a large party in the kingdom, and at prefent fo generally adopted, are founded in truth, I cannot fee how *caufes* which have a *falutary effect* among us, fhould operate as *poifon* to our neighbours; and I have a *better* opinion of the policy of the National Affembly in iffuing their *affignats*, from the *ftrong* and *violent oppofition* which was made to the meafure by their *enemies*.

It muft not be forgot, that, among the other œconomical regulations of the National Affembly, that which has taken place in their *lift* of *penfioners*, falls equally with other of their acts, under the feverity of Mr. Burke's pen. The amount of the public money given to this defcription of people by the court, was indeed *enormous*; and if we may give credit to the *Red Book*, publifhed by authority, there was *little* of the principles of *reafon* or *juftice* in the admeafurement of rewards to individuals, unlefs the *ftate* and the *country* are confidered as *feparate interefts* in the account; and that the pleafing or gratifying the *prince* and his *favourites* fhould be reckoned in the value of an *hundred pounds*

pounds to a *penny*, when set in the balance of *blood shed* in *defence* of the *nation.*

What indeed can escape Mr. Burke's censure, or what act of the French legislature can please him, (but the dissolving themselves, and leaving the king and the nobles to form their own rules of power), when he finds subject for *reproach* even in their acts of *sympathy* to the *indigent* part of the *citizens?* That Paris was always crowded with a numerous herd of mendicants, even more numerous, if possible, than those who infest and disgrace our capital, is certain; and should their numbers have encreased by the desertion of those opulent citizens who are out of temper with the government, it would neither be a *surprizing* nor an *alarming* circumstance: But it is an evil that time alone can cure, when the shock of so important a revolution has spent its force, and when the *ill humour* which at present rages in the breasts of the discontented shall subside, and lead them to return into the bosom of their country, and under the protecting laws of a regular government.

In

In a very elaborate defence of all the artificial modes of greatnefs which have taken place in fociety, Mr. Burke has ufed all the powers of eloquence and fubtlety to prove, that the crimes which have been committed by our fpecies, have not arifen from the imperfections of inftitutions, but from the vices of individuals. In *one fenfe*, his argument will be found to be *juft*; in *another*, *nugatory:* For though it muft be acknowledged, that the crimes committed by Nero proceeded from the depravity of his character, yet the *opportunity* of committing thofe crimes, and perhaps that very *depravity* of fentiment from whence they proceeded, lay in the *vice* of the *imperial inftitution.*

With the fame flow of eloquence, and the fame fubtlety, Mr. Burke recommends in all legiflators, that *tardy* caution which fuffers the *fpirit of reform to evaporate* before their work is half-finifhed; " for the evils latent in the moft promifing contrivances," fays Mr. Burke, " fhould be provided for as they arife ; one advantage is as little as poffible to be facrificed to another; for thus we compenfate, we reconcile, we balance, we are enabled

enabled to unite in a confiftent whole, the various anomalies and contending principles that are found in the minds and affairs of men."

This *finely* imagined theory would undoubtedly be adopted by all wife and good legiflators, did it in any manner fuit with the *nature* of mankind, and that *leaven* of *felfifhnefs* which taints *every principle* of human conduct. That perfect knowledge of human affairs, which Mr. Burke conceives, and juftly conceives, ought to be infeparable from the office of legiflation, will convince men, that when new conftitutions are to be formed, it is neceffary they fhould, in their formation, be regulated in all their circumftances by thofe principles which the legiflators conceive to be *the beft;* for if any thing which may be thought *defective* is left for the wifdom of future legiflators to *correct,* the conftitution muft *remain defective,* as future reformers will find their *difficulties encreafe,* inftead of being *diminifhed,* by time. The reafon is plain; for that which conftitutes the *defects* in all governments, are thofe principles in them which fupport a *partial intereft,*

to

to the injury of a *public one;* and the *prescrip-tion of time* with the *politic use of power,* has been found an *irresistible barrier* to every important part *of reformation* in the ordinary course of things.

The French legislature, in order to extin-guish those local prejudices and provincial jealousies which formerly existed in the king-dom of France, arising from the different laws and customs which took place when the in-dependent principalities were annexed to the crown; and also to regulate the rights of election in such a manner, as whilst it secured to the citizens at large this invaluable blessing, it should provide for the public tranquillity; conceived and executed a plan of dividing the kingdom into eighty-one departments. Each of these departments are divided into smaller districts, called *Communes;* and these again into smaller districts, called *Cantons.* The primary assemblies of the *cantons* elect deputies to the *communes,* one for every two hundred qualified inhabitants. The *communes* chosen by the *cantons* chuse to the *depart-ments,* and the deputies of the *departments* chuse the deputies to the *National Assembly.*

A qua-

A qualification to the right of election in the firſt inſtance, is placed at the low rate of the price of three days labour ; the qualification of being elected into the *Commune*, is the amount of ten days labour ; and that of being elected a deputy to the *National Aſſembly*, is only *one* mark of ſilver.

This plan, in theory at leaſt, promiſes to unite the higheſt degree of *freedom* with the higheſt degree of *order* : it extends the right of election *to every man who is not a pauper*, and as ſuch, by living on the *alms* of ſociety, cannot reaſonably have a *right* to enjoy its political privileges ; and whilſt it thus en-courages induſtry, by rendering it a neceſſary quality to enjoy theſe privileges, it opens the door to every man of ability to obtain the higheſt honours of his country. But this plan, ſo plauſible at leaſt in its appearance, and ſo exactly agreeing with the rights of the citizens in the *ſtricteſt ſenſe* of the word, is criticiſed by Mr. Burke in a manner *highly unworthy* of his great abilities, becauſe he deſcends to the *arts* of a quibbling ſophiſtry. He accuſes the legiſlature of not attending to their avowed principles of the equal rights of

L   men,

men, in *refuſing* their *paupers* a vote. He
aſſerts that the right of election granted in
the firſt inſtance, is no privilege at all; and
he foreſees, that the moſt *fatal diſſenſions* will
ariſe from regulations which ſeemingly tend
to *harmoniſe* every jarring principle in the
ſtate, to ſubdue every prejudice of the mind
hoſtile to the public welfare, and to combine
all its affections in the character of a loyal
citizen.

In oppoſition to Mr. Burke's accuſation, that
the legiſlature, in the qualifications they have
annexed to the rights of election, have acted
in contradiction to their avowed principles
of the equal rights of men, I ſhall, without
ſheltering myſelf under the cover of a practical uſe, (which may be uſed to juſtify every
mode of tyranny), aſſert, that the French
legiſlature have, in thoſe qualifications, ad-
hered to the rights of men in the *ſtricteſt
ſenſe*, even as they exiſt in their *abſtract* perfection in a ſtate of nature: for, who ever
conceived, that, in a ſtate of nature, a man
who was either not inclined, or by bodily
infirmity not able, to till the ground, had a
right to the fruits produced by the labour of
others?

others? In this cafe, either in a ftate of nature, or in a ftate of fociety, the *right* of maintenance depends alone on the *laws of humanity*, proceeding from that fympathy which the benevolent Author of our being has for the *beft purpofes* woven into the mental conftitution of all his *moral* creatures. But thefe laws of humanity do not oblige men to yield rights with the *donation of alms*, and to put thofe whom their charity has relieved, into a fituation of *forcing* from them the fruits of their induftry. It is on the bafis of *induftry* alone, the *only* principle which exactly fquares with a native right, and *not on rent-rolls*, that the legiflature has formed the rights of reprefentation; and this on fuch liberal principles, that every man who has activity and induftry, may qualify himfelf as to the matter of property, for a feat in the legiflative affembly. As to the nature and operation of the privileges annexed to the firft and fecond fteps in the gradation, I conceive that the regular degrees, which directly point to the grand privilege of chufing the reprefentatives, whilft they totally prevent *confufion*, and the errors of a *blind* choice,

do

do not, in *any* refpect, render *nugatory* the right of its more *abstract* principle. For every man in the Canton makes *his choice* of a deputy whom he thinks qualified by merit to reprefent him in the Commune, and *every* voter in the Commune has alfo *his choice* of a deputy to reprefent him in the department, who have a right to the choice of reprefen‑ tatives.

As Mr. Burke has made it a point to object to *every* part of the French conftitution as it now ftands, and to every act of the legifla‑ ture which refpects this conftitution, I muft follow him through all his objections, and ftate thofe reafons which appear to me to have regulated their conduct. It is true that a fenate, or an affembly of men who have had fome controul over the voice of the peo‑ ple, fome power of mitigating, regulating, or carrying into execution their laws, has always had a place in the ancient republics: But Mr. Burke himfelf feems to allow, that they are not *abfolutely* neceffary in monarchies, or rather in any government which admits of a *ftanding permanent* executive power. It is true they appear to have been a neceffary in‑ ftitution

ftitution in the ancient republics ; yet hiftory will fhew us, that their tendency has ever been *hoftile* to the principles of democracy, and often ended in the *ruin* of freedom. To the *pride*, the *avarice*, and *corruption* of the Roman Senate, was undoubtedly owing the fubverfion of the republic. It is, I think, very little to the purpofe of enlightening men's minds on the fubject of modern government, to quote the reflections of ancient authors, or draw comparifons from ancient times, which were totally unacquainted with that *excellent* policy, by which the people's power is reprefented, and brought into regular action through the means of deputation. An affembly of men *thus appointed*, feems to unite in it all the energy and fitnefs to the affairs of government of the Roman Senate, in its moft brilliant and perfect ftate, without the *latent* principles of *corruption* and *deftruction* which lurked in this inftitution.

What Lord Bolingbroke could mean I know not, when he fays, that he prefers a monarchy to other governments ; becaufe every defcription of a republic can be better engrafted on it, than any thing of a monarchy

upon

upon the republican forms; unlefs he refers
to fuch a *qualified* monarchy as is confined to
the *mere* office of an executive governor, with
the *ftability* that is annexed to *hereditary defcent;* for fure it is *impoffible* to engraft a democracy on any other defcription of monarchy. If this is his Lordfhip's meaning, the
French monarchy, as it now ftands, will be
found to agree *perfe&tly* with it; and fhould
experience prove it to be defe&tive for the
want of fuch a member as a fenate, the de-
fe&t muft be fupplied with all thofe *cautious*
preventatives which experience can alone
afford.

The *limitations* of power, in which the executive magiftrate is confined, affords Mr.
Burke a fubje&t for the exertion of *all* the
powers of his oratory. He *deplores* the mor-
tified ftate of the fallen monarch; he fees nothing but *weaknefs* in the government, and
confufion in the affairs of the empire; from
the want of a *proper influencing power in the
executive, and that cordiality which ought to
fubfift between it and the legiflative.* He conceives, that without fuch a *controuling* influence, the executive office is a ftate of *degrada-
tion,*

tion, to which *no man of spirit* would submit. And if the present King and his successors respect their *true* glory, they will take *every* opportunity which time may present, of shaking off the yoke of their imperious masters, and resuming their former independence.

To these animadversions of Mr. Burke, it may be observed, that most of the limitations of which he complains, are either *inseparable* to the security of the democracy, or they have their grounds in a *just policy*, suiting itself to the present state of things. It is necessary that a popular legislature should be informed through *other channels* than the *executive power*, of such matters as may import that body to know: it is necessary that all the means by which *a personal influence* may be established by the *grant of lands* and *large pensions*, should be taken away; and for the same reasons of policy, it is necessary that the executive power *should not* be capable of *deluding the imaginations* of men, by creating *artificial distinctions* among them.

According to Mr. Burke's political creed, Kings are only to *respect those* who serve their

I

perfonal greatnefs; and it is his opinion, that the fucceffors to the throne of France in the Bourbon line, *muft*, unlefs they are *illiterate men*, act on a principle *hoftile* to the conftitution which *they are fworn* to preferve. It is true, as Mr. Burke obferves, this is *nature;* but are not thofe very *inclinations,* fo inherent in man, the grounds for that *jealoufy* which reflecting patriots entertain *of all perfons* vefted with the dangerous gift of *permanent* authority? And unlefs the prefent monarch of France, and his fucceffors, fhall conceive *very different ideas of glory* than they will *learn* from Mr. Burke; unlefs they fhall conceive that the executing an office *faithfully*, reflects *more honour* upon them than any encreafe of *perfonal greatnefs* they can gain by *treachery;* there is very little probability that they will obtain from a popular legiflature, that enlargement of power * which may reafonably be given, when circumftances fhall *convince* the public mind that there are no grounds for jealoufy.

Mr. Burke extends his *commiferation not only* to the perfon of the King and his royal

---

* Such as the full exercife of the *Veto*.

iffue,

iffue, but *even* to the minifters of the crown in their civil capacity. In this commiferation, he *reprobates* a principle which is held out to the people of Great Britain as the grand *palladium* of their liberties, I mean the principle of refponfibility; though the reprobation is indeed qualified by a diftinction of *active* and *zealous* fervice, and the reftraint of crimes. But it is a diftinction which I cannot well underftand; for if refponfibility does not go to every part of a minifter's conduct, in which he acts without due authority, it is indeed a *very* flight conftitutional barrier againft the *vices* of adminiftration, efpecially when it is allowed among the prerogatives of our Kings, that they may chufe their own fervants, and retain them in their office at pleafure: but will any minifter who ferves fuch a King (fays Mr. Burke, when fpeaking of the prefent King of France) with but a decent appearance of refpect, *cordially* obey the orders of thofe whom but the other day in his name they had committed to the Baftille? Will they obey the orders of thofe whom, whilft they were exercifing *defpotic juftice* upon them, they conceived they were treating with

M   *lenity,*

lenity, and for whom, in a *prifon*, they thought they had provided an *afylum*.

This is faying *very little*, either for the difpofition of the minifters, or for the *fpirit* and *principles* of the ancient government. Nor can I fee that thefe gentlemen have any *reafonable* complaints to make againft the conduct of the French legiflature. It is true they are denied a feat amongft them; but this exception is not made on any *perfonal* ground: they do not except againft the abilities of thefe gentlemen, or their honefty as individuals; but they will *not* permit, either a *real*, or a *fuppofed influence*, to controul their own actions. They wi not permit that the fanctuary, in which he Majefty of the people of France refides, fhould be *polluted* or *impeached* by any *fufpicion of corruption*; and they will not endanger the liberties of their country, by giving *abfolute power any motive*, which, in the event of things, may poffibly tend to an *abufe* of *truft*.

The opinion which Mr. Burke endeavours to eftablifh in his elaborate Reflections on the French Revolution, is the *incompatibility* of a truly popular government with the human

4   conftitution:

conftitution : And the fubject which affords
him the moft ample fcope for the difplay of
his argumentative powers, is found in the
inveftment of that military force which is neceffary to the fupport of all governments;
for if that force is trufted to the people at
large, they may be tempted to act in their natural capacity, and, by deftroying or weak-
ening the energy of thofe organs by which
regular councils are held and enforced, induce a ftate of anarchy. And if the fupport of
the government is made to fubfift in a regular
ftanding difciplined body, under the controul
of an individual, that individual will become
the *mafter of the people*, and *violate* the government he was appointed to *defend*.

Either the eftablifhment or the overthrow
of an opinion fo fatal to the proud hopes of
man, muft be left to time and experience;
for I am forry to fay, that we have no notices
on which we can attempt the conftruction of
an oppofite argument. We cannot venture
to eftablifh an opinion on the ftate of a country not yet recovered from the convulfive
ftruggles which every important revolution
muft occafion. We can gain no light from
hiftory; for hiftory furnifhes *no example* of

any

any government in a large empire, which, in the ftricteft fenfe of the word, has fecured to the citizen the *full* enjoyment of his rights. Some attempts indeed have been made of this kind; but they have hitherto failed, through the *treachery* of leaders, or by the *rafh folly* of the multitude. But though thefe circumftances will prevent cautious perfons from giving a *decided* opinion on what may be the event of things, yet they do not fo *benight* the underftanding as to deprive the mind of hope. They do not prevent it from feeing that the prefent complexion of things in France has fomething of a different afpect from what hiftory, or the ftate of other countries, prefents to our view. Inftead of that *barbarous ignorance*, or that *depravity* of *principle*, which are to be feen in other European States, and which might reafonably prevent the patriot from beftowing (if it were in his power) the full boon of liberty, we fee a people *firm* and *united* in their efforts to *fupport* their rights, yet obedient * to the dictates of that government

* Mr. Burke acknowledges this obedience, and calls it *fanaticifm.*

which

which they have appointed to defend them.

From what can this difference which sub-sifts between the French nation and other societies arise, but in a more *general* diffusion of *knowledge*, and in a principle of action which consults the *public* good, as well as the gratifications of *self?* It is the business of *knowledge* to teach men their *real interests*; and it is to be hoped it will so far prevail over that *mist* which *inordinate* affections cast over the mind, as to enable the French municipalities to see, that if they so far *abuse* the power with which they have been invested for the defence of their rights, as to gratify a *private* passion at the expence of the *public* peace, they will induce a *necessity* which will lead to their *utter* destruction. It is to be hoped also, that a *true* sense of interest will enable the army to perceive, that the *moment they fling off the character of the citizen, and assume a controuling power over their country*, from that moment they become *individually slaves*; for the very circumstance in their condition by which this power must subsist, is a discipline inseparable to the

strictest

ſtricteſt ſubordination, and which in *all* re-
ſpects muſt militate againſt their civil rights.
When the Roman army was in the very
height of their power; when it was enabled
to depoſe and murder emperors, and raiſe
private men to the imperial throne; when
they were enabled to ravage the empire at
their pleaſure, and exact largeſſes from its
ſpoils; they were, in an *individual* capacity,
the *greateſt* of ſlaves.

The patriot Frenchman has a proſpect of
hope which *never* yet offered itſelf to the
view of ſociety, and that is in the *diſintereſtedneſs* of thoſe councils to which he has
confided his right. The republican parliament of England, by their *inordinate* thirſt
after public offices, and by uſing their power
to their *own emolument*, gave *too much room*
for the ſuſpicions of a divided people to act
in their diſfavour; and it muſt be acknow_
ledged, that the intereſts of ſelf have been
obſerved to act as much in popular councils
as in courts. But the French legiſlature have
ſet, in this point, an example *unparellelled* in
the hiſtory of man. To a *bold* and *enterpriſ-
ing* ſpirit, they have united a *diſintereſtedneſs*

of

of principle which has deprived their enemies of *every* means of oppofition, but *vain*
declamation, *groundlefs* accufation, and *impo-
tent* hope. Long may they continue the
admiration of the world in thefe important
particulars! Long may they thus continue
to *aggrandize* the character of man! And
long may they continue to deferve a *monument of efteem* on the minds of their fpecies,
which neither *time,* nor *accident,* nor *adverfe
fortune, fhall be able to efface!*

It cannot be denied that Mr. Burke has
made a difplay of very *uncommon* abilities in
his attack on the French Revolution; but
why has he deigned to make ufe of the
mean arts of abufe as an *auxiliary* in the
conteft? Why has he, by the moft *invidious*
comparifons, and *groundlefs* accufations, endeavoured to roufe all nations and all defcriptions of men againft them, and thus to
crufh in their ruin all the rights of man? Is
the tendency of his publication a *recommen-
dation* to the Britifh government, to dragoon
their neighbours into an adoption of their
own fyftem of policy? Would he recommend

commend to the potentates of Europe, a renewal of that *wicked conspiracy* againſt the rights of men, which was planned by Henry the Fourth and his miniſter Sully, and which was only prevented from taking place by the timely death of that monarch? —a plan, by which, through the *combination* of power, modes of government were to be *arbitrarily* impoſed and ſupported, and the rights of conſcience *aboliſhed*. If ſuch *violent* councils were indeed to take place of that *moderation* and *equity* which has hitherto been ſhewn, it would *prove* that the *forming treaties* and directing the *force of nations* were but *ill* truſted to the *ſecrecy* of cabinets. When we reflect that ſuch dreadful purpoſes can never be effected without the effuſion of *oceans* of blood, of ſuch an invidious intention we muſt certainly exculpate Mr. Burke; unleſs, by a *ſtrange* modification of *ſympathy*, the lives of plebeians, and thoſe vulgar characters which compoſe the " *ſwiniſh multitude*," is held at *no value* in his account. Some of Mr. Burke's expreſſions, indeed, ſeem to warrant us in making ſuch a ſuppoſition, though we *muſt acknowledge*, that, in

others,

others, he appears to have a *concern* for the
spiritual, if not for the *temporal* happinefs of
thofe he defpifes: "Whilft, fays he, the wealth
and pride of individuals at every moment
makes the man of humble rank and fortune
fenfible of his inferiority, and *degrades* and
vilifies his condition*; it is for the man in
humble life, and to raife his nature, and to
put him in mind of a ftate in which the
privileges of opulence will ceafe, when he
will be equal by nature, and may be more
than equal by virtue, that this portion of the
general wealth of his country is employed,
and fanctified."

If Mr. Burke, in the management of his
argument, could have defcended from the
lofty ftrain of a *poetic* imagination, to the *drud-
gery* of clofe reafoning, he would have perceived the *error* of deviating from the line of
expediency into the queftion of *right* ; for

---

* This is a fad condition, indeed, for "*naked fhivering
nature* :" But what is the remedy ? why, let them refpect
property, and feek "their confolation in the final pro-
portions of eternal juftice." *Vide* Reflections, page 147
and 351.

N   when

when we once *give up* the point, that there is an *inherent* right attached to privileged perfons to make laws for the community, we cannot fix on any other principle that will ftand the teft of argument, but the *native* and *unalienable* rights of man. For if we fay that *lawful* governments are formed on the authority of conventions, it will be afked, *who gave thefe conventions their authority?* If we grant that they derived their authority from the *affent of the people*, how came the people, it will be faid, to exert fuch an authority at *one* period of fociety, and not at *another?* If we fay it was *neceffity* that recovered to the focial man the full rights of his nature, it will be afked, *who is to be the judge* of this neceffity? why *certainly* the people.

Thus, in *every* light in which we can place the argument, in every poffible mode of reafoning, we fhall be driven back to elect either the firft or the fecond of thefe propofitions; either that an individual, or fome privileged perfons, have an inherent and indefeafible right to make laws for the community, or that this authority refts in the unalienable and indefeafible rights of man.

That

That the people have often abufed their power, it muft be granted; for they have often *facrificed* themfelves and their pofterity to the *wanton will* of an individual, and *this* is the foundation of all the regal tyrannies which have fubfifted in fociety; but *no abufe* of their power can *take away their right*, becaufe their right *exifts in the very conftitution of things.* If the French people therefore fhould be fo *capricious* as to fling off their new conftitution, and fubject themfelves to more *unequal* forms of government, or even to *tyranny*, it will be agreeable to the courfe of paft experience: but fuch an exertion of power *cannot injure their right*; and whatever form or complexion any future government in France may bear, it can have no *legitimate* fource, *but in the will of the people.*

> I am,
>> My Lord,
>>> With great efteem and refpect,
>>>> Your Lordfhip's
>>>>> Moft obedient
>>>>> Humble Servant,
>>>>>> The AUTHOR.